CELINE

Marianne McKay

MetroBooks

DION

MetroBooks

An Imprint of Friedman/Fairfax Publishers

Library of Congress Cataloging-in-Publication Data available upon request.

ISBN 1-56799-864-X

Editor: Emily Zelner
Art Director: Jeff Batzli
Designer: Liz Trovato
Photography Editor: Valerie E. Kennedy
Production Manager: Camille Lee

Color separations by Radstock Repro
Printed in England by Butler and Tanner, Ltd.

1 3 5 7 9 10 8 6 4 2

For bulk purchases and special sales,
please contact: Friedman/Fairfax Publishers
Attention: Sales Department
15 West 26th Street
New York, NY 10010
212/685-6610   FAX 212/685-1307

Visit our website:
http://www.metrobooks.com

Above: *Céline at the Grammy rehearsals in New York in February 1998.*

Opposite: *Performing is second nature to Céline who's been singing before live audiences since she was a little girl. So she is no newcomer to the throngs of fans and reporters who greet her wherever she goes. Here she gives a big thumbs up to the camera.*

Below: Since she was five years old, Céline has had only one dream: to sing. The joy she takes in singing is as evident today as it was in this photo of her in the early 1990's.

Opposite: Céline has told interviewers that she and René are serious about taking time off in the near future, and that she intends to do all sorts of ordinary but pleasurable things that most people take for granted—driving her car, cooking, and most of all, trying to have a baby.

CONTENTS

Céline never takes her gifts for granted; she studies each song, practices her voice exercises, and puts all her concentration into each effort, be it in the studio or on stage. She says that each time she sings a song, she experiences the emotions that she felt upon first hearing it.

Above: *Always interested in fashion, Céline has a special fondness for Chanel. When she gets the chance, she attends a runway show.*

Opposite: *Céline receives about a thousand songs a year from aspiring and successful songwriters alike. Her staff members review each submission, looking for the special songs that will touch Céline's heart. Of that number, she actually chooses to record about twelve to fifteen songs.*

INTRODUCTION

The Setting: Late 1970s, Le Vieux Baril (The Old Barrel), a piano bar and restaurant in Charlemagne, Quebec, a small town about a half an hour's drive east of Montreal.

The Audience: Every night, a sell-out crowd of wildly enthusiastic Québécois, drawn not only from surrounding towns but from all over the province, to hear "the little girl with the big voice."

The Singer: A thin, petite girl, perhaps ten years old, belting out a mix of traditional songs and the hits of a popular Quebec chanteuse named Ginette Reno—and dreaming of becoming a star.

Flash forward to the Academy Awards ceremony, March 1998. In front of a live audience of Hollywood stars and powerbrokers packing the famed Shrine Auditorium, plus more than a billion television viewers tuning in around the world, Céline Dion takes the stage to sing her mega-hit "My Heart Will Go On," the theme from the movie *Titanic*. Attired in a Halston gown and sporting a $2.2 million replica of the movie's "Heart of the Sea" diamond and sapphire pendant, she belts out the song in her signature dramatic style. The theme from *Titanic* wins Best Original Song (one of a record-matching eleven Oscars for the movie), and Céline attends the post-ceremony parties, taking the glamorous company and legendary surroundings in stride. After all, she is the world's most popular female singer. Céline's signature song "My Heart Will Go On" is the most frequently played song in the history of American radio.

Just how did that girl from Charlemagne achieve such heights of superstardom? Here is her incredible story of talent, hard work, and luck…

Above: *Wearing Chanel, one of her favorite labels, Céline posed for photographers in Monaco, where she was attending the World Music Awards.*

Opposite: *Of the process of selecting a song, Céline says, "I have to have tears in my eyes myself before asking you to be moved by it."*

Above: *The Time for Peace Awards, New York City, November 17, 1997.*

Opposite: *Who could have predicted that this little girl, pictured here at age four in a snap-shot taken in a Woolworth's photo booth, would grow up to be the world's hottest diva?*

CHAPTER ONE

THE LITTLE GIRL WITH THE BIG VOICE

Born the fourteenth child in a family for which music was an essential part of life, Céline Dion was practically destined to be a talented singer. But no one could have predicted that a girl from such humble beginnings would rise to the pinnacle of world stardom.

In the summer of 1944, at a community dance in the small town of La Tuque, Quebec, eighteen-year old Thérèse Tanguay picked up a violin and began to play "Le Reel de Sainte Anne," a popular folk tune. Inspired, a young man named Adhémar Dion (who hoped to become a musician) joined in on the accordion. Brought together by music, the

Five-year-old Céline (left, front) poses with family members at her brother Michel's wedding in 1973. As the youngest of all her siblings Céline received the special honor of being the flower girl in the ceremony.

two young people quickly fell in love, marrying just ten months later. Coincidentally, both Thérèse and Adhémar had grown up in the farming community of Sainte-Anne-des-Monts in Quebec's Gaspé region, though they never met until hard times had forced both families off their farms to seek work in the more prosperous town of La Tuque.

The newly married couple welcomed their first child, Denise, in 1946. By the summer of 1952, Thérèse had given birth to four more children, and the family was struggling to make ends meet. The promise of a job in a factory drew the Dions to the town of Charlemagne,

Eight-year-old Céline at home in Charlemagne, Canada.

situated some thirty miles (50km) east of Montreal. Adhémar worked eighteen hours a day just to keep food on the table and pay the rent on their small apartment, and he and Thérèse soon began to yearn for the simple pleasures of the farm life that they had left behind. Determined to build a better life for their growing family, the couple scrimped and saved (Adhémar walked to and from the factory every day) until they were able to put a small down payment on some land.

Having used all their funds to buy the land, Thérèse and Adhémar lacked the money to pay a builder. So close to achieving their goal, they decided to forge ahead and build the house themselves. With Thérèse pregnant with their seventh child and Adhémar still working overtime at the factory, they nevertheless devoted every spare moment to their new home, hammering late into the night, until it was done. That same sense of discipline and stubborn determination to achieve one's goals were passed on to their children, and to this day, Céline cites her parents' work ethic as central to her own success.

The other quality that the Dion parents passed on to all their children was a profound love of music. The Dion household was always filled with music, as each child played an instrument (or more than one) and sang. Friends and neighbors were always welcome to join in, and on weekends the cozy farmhouse was frequently the scene of music and laughter-filled jam sessions that lasted long into the night.

On March 30, 1968, Thérèse gave birth to the couple's fourteenth, and last, child, a girl, whom they named after a favorite song, "Céline." With thirteen musical siblings, it was no wonder that

Céline learned to sing almost as soon as she could talk. When she was just a little girl, the family formed a group—The Dion Family—that performed at community events. It was soon obvious that Céline had a special talent. Her sisters and brothers encouraged Céline to sing, and soon the child was practicing the moves she'd seen the pros perform on television. At the age of five, Céline made her public debut, singing three songs at her brother Michel's wedding, one of which was the traditional "Du fil, des aiguilles, et du coton" (Thread, Needles, and Cotton).

This tiny child with a natural five-octave range could belt out the tunes with passion even then, and everyone in the church that day recalls her performance with awe. That event is accepted as the moment when the family knew that Céline would be a star. Just how far she would go, however, no one could have predicted.

Child Prodigy

In the mid-seventies, Thérèse and Adhémar decided to undertake a new business venture. They opened Le Vieux Baril, a restaurant and piano bar, in Charlemagne. A true family business, it featured Thérèse in the kitchen, Adhémar as the manager, and the Dion kids doing double duty as waiters and entertainers.

Céline was attending school in the daytime and helping out at the club in the evenings. She has told many interviewers that she found school difficult. Teased by the other kids because of her prominent front teeth, and bored with her schoolwork, Céline took refuge in daydreams about becoming a star. Céline was a natural performer, and her powerful voice and emotional delivery made her the main act at Le Vieux Baril. She performed a mixture of traditional folk tunes and contemporary pop, with an emphasis on the songs of Ginette Reno, a hugely popular Quebec chanteuse whose hits Céline regularly practiced at home in front of a mirror.

It wasn't long before Le Vieux Baril was packed with customers every night, many of whom were drawn to hear "the little girl with the big voice." It was clear that Céline loved every minute she was on stage—singing was all she thought about. Her mother recalled that Céline would cry if denied the opportunity to perform at the restaurant. And her performances not infrequently brought her audience to tears. Though she was barely ten years old, Céline had already developed the warmth and poise on stage that characterize her performances today.

Opposite: *Céline, at age twelve, takes center stage in this photograph of the entire Dion family.*

Below: *A class picture taken during the 1979-80 school year.*

As Céline continued to draw crowds (who now came from all over Quebec to hear her sing), it became clear to the Dion family that their youngest member was meant for something bigger. She had an incredible talent, and though she was rapidly becoming a local celebrity, the little town of Charlemagne could not hold much of a future. Though they were approached by various managers, and Céline did perform some gigs in other small towns, the family was not sure how to proceed. When she was twelve years old, her family decided to act.

Working with Jacques, Céline's older brother and an avid supporter of his sister's dreams, Thérèse wrote a song entitled "Ce n'était qu'un rêve" (It Was Only a Dream). Using an inexpensive, borrowed tape recorder, Thérèse taped Céline's rendition of the song, while Jacques accompanied her on guitar. On the back of a Ginette Reno album they found the name and address of Reno's manager, a Montreal-based former singing star named René Angélil. Wrapping the tape in a red ribbon and adding a note that said "This is a twelve-year-old with a fantastic voice....We want her to be like Ginette Reno," Thérèse sent the package to Angélil.

Above: Céline makes her public debut in June of 1981 at age thirteen on a popular Canadian talk show hosted by Michel Jasmin. She and Michel display her first record to go gold.

Opposite: Céline with her niece Karine Menard at age thirteen.

The Discovery

In January 1981, when René Angélil first heard of Céline Dion, he was at a low point in a career that had seen better years. Born on January 16, 1942, René had grown up one of two sons in a working class family in Montreal. By all accounts a good student, René was also interested in singing, and formed a band, Les Baronnets, with two classmates. Modeling themselves on The Beatles, Les Baronnets began performing in clubs and soon became popular. They attracted the attention of a manager named Ben Kaye, who helped them polish their act and booked them into major venues, including Atlantic City's Steel Pier. By the mid-sixties, Les Baronnets were stars in Quebec.

In 1973, tired of the stress of performing and with a divorce behind him (the marriage had resulted in one son), René retired from performing to become a manager like Ben Kaye. Although it was a difficult business, René eventually had a number of notable successes among his clientele, including a teenage heart-throb named René Simard and Céline's idol, Ginette Reno. Always a gambler, René had invested almost his entire savings in Reno's career and had been rewarded when she became one of Quebec's most popular singers. However, in November 1980 he was shocked to receive a telephone call from Reno telling him he was fired. He had married again, to Anne, with whom he had two children, and although Anne had a successful career of her own—she appeared in a popular television show called *Les Tannants* (The Troublemakers)—it was

CELINE AND THE CYSTIC FIBROSIS FOUNDATION

Céline is a tireless fundraiser and advocate for the Canadian Cystic Fibrosis Foundation. The disease has touched her personally, having claimed the life of her sixteen-year-old niece, Karine (the daughter of Céline's sister Liette), in 1993. Starting in 1982, Céline became a vocal supporter of the cause, performing benefits; donating concert fees; giving a portion of profits from her restaurant chain, Nickels; and appearing on television (most recently in November 1998, when she performed on the show *Touched by an Angel*). The song *"Vol"* (Fly), on the album *D'eux*, is dedicated to Karine.

THE FAMILY DION

Céline is extremely close to her family.
Here are their names and birthdates:

PARENTS

Adhémar	**March 2, 1923**
Thérèse	**March 20, 1927**

SIBLINGS

Denise	**August 16, 1946**
Clément	**November 2, 1947**
Claudette	**December 10, 1948**
Liette	**February 8, 1950**
Michel	**August 18, 1952**
Louise	**September 22, 1953**
Jacques	**March 10, 1955**
Daniel	**November 29, 1956**
Ghislaine	**July 28, 1958**
Linda	**June 23, 1959**
Manon	**October 7, 1960**
Paul	**April 3, 1962**
Pauline	**April 3, 1962**

Opposite, top: The family Dion in the early nineties.

Opposite, bottom: Céline with her two greatest supporters, Dad and Mom.

nonetheless a bad time for René to be facing financial difficulties.

The next events have become part of the Céline Dion legend. When René received the tape, one of hundreds sent to him over the years by young hopefuls, he expected very little. Upon listening to it, however, he has said that he received "the shock of my artistic life." Grabbing the telephone, he called Thérèse and arranged for a meeting.

When Céline walked into René's office, a shy, skinny twelve-year-old wearing a dress handsewn for the occasion by her mother, she was terribly nervous. René asked her to sing, and when she said that she was used to using a microphone, he handed her a pen, and told her to pretend she was in front of an audience. Bolstered by her mother's reassuring advice, "Just be yourself," Céline shut her eyes and began to sing. As the emotion-filled strains of "Ce n'était qu'un rêve" began to fill his office, René was stunned. Moved to tears, René signed Céline on the spot, telling her mother "I will make her a star."

Above: *Céline was in New York City for the official release of her fifth English album,* Let's Talk About Love, *on November 16, 1997. Here, photographers caught her the next evening as she attended the Time for Peace party; the following morning she appeared on the* Rosie O'Donnell Show.

Opposite: *A young Céline posed for this publicity photo.*

CHAPTER TWO

LA P'TITE QUÉBÉCOISE

René was unshakable in his faith not only in Céline's talent, but also in his ability to guide her to stardom. The challenge lay in convincing everyone else.

First, he persuaded Céline's parents to let him take charge of her life, arranging for piano lessons, hiring a well-known Quebec singing coach to work with the young girl, and even asking his wife to pass on tips about performing in front of the camera. Next, unable to drum up commercial financing, he persuaded Anne to let him mortgage their home in order to finance Céline's debut.

René decided to send Céline into the studio to record two albums, which he would produce himself. He hired songwriters (including Eddy Marnay, who had written songs for Barbra Streisand, Edith Piaf, and Nana Mouskouri, among others), arrangers (including Daniel Hétu, Ginette Reno's bandleader), and studio musicians, and oversaw each recording personally. A song by Marnay, who had described Céline as being able to sing with God's own voice, provided the name of one album, *La Voix du Bon Dieux,* which was to be a collection of emotional ballads (including Thérèse's "Ce n'était qu'un rêve"). The other album, *Céline Chante Noël,* would feature a variety of Christmas tunes.

By June 1981, after more than a year of hard work, René decided Céline was ready for her public debut. Using connections from a lifetime in show business, René persuaded the powers behind Quebec's most popular talk show, hosted by Michel Jasmin, to let Céline appear. On June 19, Jasmin introduced Céline as a "hot new young talent with a magnificent voice." The trembling thirteen-year-old took the stage, and from the moment the first notes hit them, the audience was hers.

That was the beginning of Quebec's love for Céline, an affection that she has always returned whole-heartedly.

Above: *Céline works out regularly to keep herself in fantastic shape, which is shown off by this clingy dress.*

Opposite: *All in white, Céline is a dramatic figure on stage.*

A Star in the Making

In the autumn of 1981, the albums were ready for release. Céline began to follow a grueling schedule of autographings at record stores, television and radio appearances, live concerts, and even visits to speak to schoolchildren—ironic, because by this point, her own schooling had been largely discontinued. René did hire a tutor to ensure that Céline met the basic requirements of a high school education, but it was hardly a priority. Rehearsals, voice lessons, and dance training were her focus.

In 1982, Céline went to France to record a third album. René had managed to convince a major French record label to sign Céline, and the album, *Tellement j'ai d'amour pour toi* (I Have So Much Love for You), won a gold record in France. Suddenly, radio stations in Quebec could not play enough Céline Dion, and the album sold more than 50,000 copies in Canada.

In yet another coup that same year, Céline was selected from a field of 2,000 entrants to perform at Tokyo's Yamaha World Popular Song Festival. One of thirty contestants asked to attend the festival, Céline sang in front of her largest live audience yet—12,000 people—with an estimated television audience of more than 100 million. Nervous, yet anxious to put all her hard work to the test, Céline performed brilliantly. "Tellement…" won the festival's Best Song award, and Céline was honored as the Best Artist.

CELINE'S VOICE REGIMEN

In 1990, persistent hoarseness sent Céline to New York-based voice specialist Dr. Gwen Korovin, who recommended complete silence for two weeks to rest the singer's overworked vocal cords. The treatment worked, but the experience forced Céline to acknowledge that her voice was a precious instrument that would require special care. Céline adopted a strict regimen. On the day of a performance, she does not speak at all, using hand signals and written notes to communicate. She is careful to humidify her rooms, and when she travels, she takes along two humidifiers. Even on days when she is not singing, Céline does a series of voice exercises. Occasionally, she will rest her voice by not speaking for twenty-four hours. Céline told *USA Today* reporter Edna Gundersen that she feels a responsibility to her fans and to herself to keep her voice in top condition. "People are expecting a lot from me. I expect a lot from me, too….The least I can do is take care of my voice."

On her return, she was publicly congratulated by the then-Premier of Quebec, René Lévesque. It was clear that Céline was becoming the darling of the province, whose French-speaking residents were proud to have an international star to call their own. She was their "p'tite québécoise."

Opposite: *Céline posed for a series of publicity shots in 1995.*

Above: *Always conscious of the major role her fans have played in her phenomenal success, Céline never fails to take a moment to flash them a smile or to sign autographs.*

A Hardworking Teenager

Determined to ride the growing wave of popularity, René made sure that Céline continued to tour and record constantly, both in Quebec and in Europe. Thérèse frequently came along on road trips. Fifteen-year-old Céline did manage to date a little, but René insisted that if she wanted to be a star, she would have to sacrifice many of the experiences that teenage girls usually enjoy, such as best girlfriends, dating, and parties. She practiced daily and viewed videos of her performances in order to identify and correct mistakes. Her regimen was strict: no late nights, no cold drinks (hard on the throat), absolutely no cigarette smoking or alcoholic beverages. Céline says that she is not particularly sorry to have missed out on the typical teenage rituals: she has wanted to be a performer ever since she can remember, she was grateful to René for mapping out her path to stardom, and she was willing to work as hard as necessary to make it happen.

What little spare time she did have was spent in the company of her always supportive and ever-growing family (her older sisters and brothers were now having children of their own, and Céline loved to spend time with her nieces and nephews.) During this time she did, however, opt to get her teeth fixed—ever since teasing children had labeled her "vampire," she had been sensitive about her teeth, even holding her hand in front of her mouth when she spoke—and now that she could afford to get the work done, she was eager to do it.

Above: *This outfit shows off Céline's newly adult image—a sheer black bejeweled top and a mane of curls were intended to give her a sexier look.*

Opposite: *Touring in support of* Unison *in 1990, Céline was already a seasoned performer, putting on the kind of show that has won her legions of loyal fans.*

The next two years passed in a rush of hard work and undreamed-of success. In 1983, Céline recorded three more albums: *Chants et contes de Noël* (Songs and Tales for Christmas), *Les chemins de ma maison* (The Paths of My House), and *Du soleil au coeur* (Sunshine in My Heart). That summer Céline appeared in concert at Lac des Dauphins in Montreal before more than 45,000 people, a concert that was recorded by Société Radio-Canada (Canada's national radio service). She performed a series of sold-out shows at Paris' famed Olympia Theatre (where celebrated chanteuse Edith Piaf had triumphed), and her single "D'amour ou d'amitié" ("Love or Friendship") sold in excess of 700,000 copies in France, making her the first Canadian to receive a gold record there. Not unexpectedly, Céline cleaned up at the Félix Awards, Quebec's equivalent of the Grammy Awards sponsored by the province's society of recording artists (ASDIQ).

Never slowing her frenetic pace, in 1984 she released the albums *Mélanie*, which went platinum (more than 100,000 copies sold), followed by *Les oiseaux du bonheur* (The Birds of Happiness), which was sold only in Europe, and a greatest hits compilation, *Les plus grands succès de Céline Dion*. That same year, Pope John Paul II came to Montreal. Devoted Catholics, the Dions were thrilled when Céline was asked to sing during the papal visit. She performed several songs before an audience of 65,000 at Montreal's Olympic Stadium.

The next year saw two more albums, *Céline Dion en concert* and *C'est pour toi* (It's For You). In the six years since she began working with René, Céline had reached the pinnacle of success for a Québécois performer. All together,

Opposite: *A proud daughter of Quebec, Céline is always very happy to perform for a home-province crowd as here at the Inauguration Theater.*

Above: *Céline met with Pope John Paul II in Rome a year after she performed for him in Montreal. She is said to have kissed the papal ring and given him a framed gold record for one of the songs she sang during his visit to Canada.*

In September 1994, Céline did a series of sold-out shows at the Olympia Theater in Paris, two of which were recorded for the Céline à l'Olympia album.

Céline's recordings over the previous three years had won a record fifteen Félix Awards. In addition to being Quebec's biggest star, Céline was an internationally recognized singer, with a number of gold albums in France. Her incessant touring had made her an incredibly polished performer for someone so young. Yet she had not grown jaded: as she matured, her delivery remained emotionally powerful and grew ever more complex. Unbelievably, all the adulation she'd received had not turned her head; Céline remained the sweet, hardworking girl whose sheer joy in singing had won the hearts of visitors to Le Vieux Baril. Her fondest hours were spent with family members, to whom she was unceasingly generous, giving her siblings gifts and buying her parents a new house near Montreal as well as a vacation home.

Céline had left school for good at sixteen. At eighteen, she remained focused on a single goal: singing stardom. True fame required that she become known outside the French-speaking world—specifically, that she make it in the United States, the world's biggest entertainment market—and that she successfully navigate the career transition from child prodigy to adult performer with true staying power. It was a daunting challenge—but René had a vision and Céline believed in it. His genius for choosing the right career moves plus Céline's incredible talent and determination made a potent combination. So René mapped out the next stage of the plan: Céline would take an unprecedented break from touring and recording during which she would learn English and revamp her image, in preparation for conquering the Anglophone world.

In 1988, two Swiss songwriters approached Céline and asked her to perform their song at the annual Eurovision Song Contest in Dublin, Ireland. In May of that year, Céline gave a bravura performance and captured the top prize for the Swiss.

Above: *Céline proudly displays her first Grammy Award, at the 1993 event on February 2nd. Céline and Peabo Bryson split the award for Best Vocal Performance by a Duo for their rendition of "Beauty and the Beast."*

Opposite: *Céline exudes an exotic look in this publicity shot.*

CHAPTER THREE

BREAKTHROUGH

After a "sabbatical" that lasted eighteen months, a "new" Céline appeared on the scene. Daily study at the Berlitz School had given her a grasp of English that, while shaky, was serviceable. Image consultants had taught her to use make-up, and shopping sprees had provided a newly sophisticated wardrobe. Her new wealth meant that Céline was able to buy whatever she wanted, and she discovered another vocation: shopping for designer clothing and shoes. She has since joked that shopping is her "sport." (By 1999, according to one interviewer, she had amassed an astonishing one thousand pairs of shoes.)

In addition to embracing a more womanly image, Céline wanted to expand her musical repertoire, adding pop songs to the list of traditional favorites and ballads that she had sung for so long.

Céline takes to the dance floor at a post-concert party in the spring of 1995.

As with everything, René had planned Céline's "comeback" carefully. He convinced a senior executive at Sony Music Canada to attend a concert in Montreal. Céline delivered an impassioned performance; the fans, having missed Céline while she was on hiatus, responded with uninhibited approval. Bowled over, the powers-that-be at Sony signed Céline to a multi-disc deal for more than $1 million.

Incognito

Céline's first album for Sony was in French; 1987's *Incognito* was welcomed by fans and shot to the top of the charts in Quebec and France, alerting Sony to the possibility that they had a singer of enormous potential on their hands. Céline was then asked to perform at the 1988 Eurovision song contest, a huge event to be held in Dublin and broadcast to more than 600 million television viewers in Europe, the (then) USSR, the Middle East, Japan, and Australia. Her winning song, "Ne partez pas sans moi," (Don't Leave Without Me), sold more than 300,000 copies in Europe alone. Céline was back—and ready to conquer the world.

At twenty years old, as she stood poised on the brink of real stardom, something else was about to change for Céline: the nature of her relationship with the most important figure in her life, René. Although she kept it secret for several years, it was at the Eurovision contest that René and Céline shared their first real kiss. René and Anne had divorced in 1985, so there was no legal impediment to Céline and René's relationship, but both were concerned that the age difference would draw negative comment. So, despite their growing love for one another, Céline and René were extremely careful to maintain a publicly platonic relationship. The two had been inseparable for years, as René exercised total control over Céline's career, so very few people noticed the difference in the way they felt about one another—at first.

Meanwhile, the time had come for Céline to record in English.

Céline dissolves into giggles at a party in 1995.

Committed to making Céline a star in the English-language market, Sony spared no expense in the production of Céline's first English album. 1990's *Unison* featured the recording genius of no fewer than three major music producers, including Canada's own David Foster, who had worked with Barbra Streisand, Céline's idol. When the album was released, Sony's publicity team burst into action, sending Céline on a major promotional blitz across the continent. English-speaking Canada embraced Céline's work, and in 1990 she won Juno Awards (Canada's Grammy) for Album of the Year and Female Vocalist of the Year. MuchMusic, Canada's music video channel, picked Céline's duet with Billy Newton-Davis, "Can't Live With You, Can't Live Without You," as a winner.

Not willing to rest with Canadian success, Céline's team continued to work for U.S. recognition. In a major coup, she was booked on *The Tonight Show*, where guest host Jay Leno introduced her as "a huge star up there in Canada." Just twenty-two years old, but already a seasoned performer, Céline delivered a splendid performance of "Where Does My Heart Beat Now?" and won hearts all across the United States. A few months later, "Where Does My Heart Beat Now?" had climbed to number 4 on the *Billboard* charts. With *Unison*, it seemed that Céline had arrived.

Céline has had the advantage of working in recording studios with a number of the world's best producers, from Sir George Martin to Canadian David Foster.

Trouble in Paradise

Back home in Quebec, some of Céline's fans were feeling betrayed by her move into the English market. Never interested in politics, their "p'tite québécoise" hastened to reassure them, saying "I love to sing in French," but, she told the press, "I want to be known....that's why I'm doing my first English album."

Francophone fans were upset further when Céline was nominated for another Félix award—in the Anglophone Artist category. Determined to put an end to the controversy, Céline declined to accept the award. Suffering from laryngitis, she took the stage to publicly profess her loyalty to her home province, announcing, "I'm proud to be a québécoise."

Proving that her words came from the heart, Céline was soon back in the studio, recording in French once again. *Dion chante Plamodon* is a tribute from one of Quebec's best loved singers to one of its legendary songwriters, Luc Plamodon. This 1991 album remains a favorite among serious Céline Dion fans because of the passion and subtlety that she conveys through Plamodon's songs.

Continuing her quest to break through in the U.S. market, Céline began work on a new album in English, to be called, simply, *Céline Dion*. Once again, a heavy-hitting producer was brought into the studio, in this case, Walter Afanasieff, who had worked with Whitney Houston and Michael Bolton. In addition, the artist formerly known as Prince, who had

Céline's European tour in 1995 included a stop at London's Wembley Stadium.

penned hits for singers like Sheena Easton and Sinead O'Connor, wrote a song called "With This Tear" for Céline. Four hit singles later ("Love Can Move Mountains," "Did You Give Enough Love," "Water From the Moon," and "If You Asked Me To"), Céline Dion was a huge success.

Opposite and below: *Céline gives an electrifying performance at Wembley Stadium.*

Disney Comes Calling

Orchestrated by René and thoroughly supported by Sony (which, eager to hang on to this potentially huge money-maker, renegotiated her contract to the tune of $10 million—an unprecedented deal for a Canadian artist), Céline's breakthrough in the U. S. market was a fait accompli. Though not yet a household name, Céline had proven herself a marketable commodity. It took Disney, that juggernaut of marketing muscle, to help Céline achieve the superstardom she yearned for.

In 1991, at the request of Steven Spielberg, who had seen Céline perform at Canada's Juno Awards, Céline recorded a song for the movie *An American Tail: Fievel Goes West*. The song was never used in the final film, but the songwriter, James Horner, took notice of Céline's superb voice, and the gig brought her to the attention of the Hollywood community. That connection led Disney executives to Céline when it was time to find a singer to duet with Peabo Bryson for the theme to Disney's new animated feature, *Beauty and the Beast*.

Peabo Bryson had had a great success with his soulful Roberta Flack duet, "Tonight, I Celebrate My Love," and Céline was thrilled to work with him. Walter Afanasieff returned to produce, and masterminded the sessions with Bryson and Céline. Disney brought its full weight to bear in promoting the movie and the song, which was nominated for an Academy Award for Best Original Song, and Céline was

Attired in a revealing red "bandage" dress, Céline posed with Peabo Bryson at the American Music Awards in January 1993. Their duet "Beauty and the Beast" had won an Oscar the previous March.

FAST FACTS

Birthdate: **March 30, 1968**
Height: **5'7" (1.7m)**
Eyes: **Brown**
Favorite (non-singing) Activity: **Shopping**
Favorite Colors: **Red, black, white**
Lucky Number: **5**
Favorite Perfume: **Chanel Number 5**
Favorite Sport: **Golf**

Céline is a polished performer who dominates the stage. Her carefully choreographed performances feature top backup talent, dramatic lighting and stage sets, designer outfits, and of course, the singer's own insistence on giving her best at every concert.

asked to perform. Her appearance at the 1992 Oscars coincided with her twenty-fourth birthday—and what better birthday present could she have received than the announcement that the Oscar for Best Original Song went to "Beauty and the Beast"? The night was a dream come true for Céline...but there were more honors to come.

To her joy, when that year's Grammy nominations were announced, Céline was nominated for Female Pop Vocalist of the Year. To make it even better, "Beauty and the Beast" was also nominated, for both Best Vocal Performance by a Duo and Record of the Year. Céline and Peabo performed the song at the awards, and though the Female Pop award went to kd lang (a fellow Canadian), Céline and Peabo were proud to (each) take home a Grammy for the Best Vocal Performance by a Duo. In March, Céline won another Juno, this time for Female Singer of the Year; and in May, Céline traveled to Monaco where she received her first World Music Award. Amidst all of this, Céline actually found the time and energy to work with megastar Michael Bolton as the opening act on his 1992 tour.

Eager to follow up on the success of her album *Céline Dion* and to work again with David Foster, who had produced *Unison*, Céline began work on her third Anglophone album. *The Colour of My Love* was titled after a song that Foster wrote for his wife, and became a favorite with Céline. She finds the song so full of love, says Céline, that she cannot always control her emotions when she sings it. Even after all the times she has performed it, the song can still bring tears to her eyes.

At the Gay Men's Health Crisis benefit, Céline gets a bear hug from long-time friend and producer David Foster. Foster said that he knew in 1991 that Céline would reach great heights. "I truly, truly believe in my heart that Céline is the world's next superstar."

The Colour of My Love also included a duet with Clive Griffin, "When I Fall in Love," which was featured in the hit movie *Sleepless in Seattle*, and a song by Jennifer Rush called "The Power of Love." The latter had been a hit in Europe, as sung by Rush herself, then was covered by several artists. When Céline heard it, she knew she could bring a special feeling to the song. Céline's version of "The Power of Love" went straight to the top of the *Billboard* Hot 100, and became Céline's first number one hit in the U.S. market. Another song, "Think Twice," became a huge success in Britain, sending the single and the album to the top position on the British charts for five weeks in a row, a feat unmatched since the Beatles did it in 1965.

Packed with the kind of all-out love songs that Céline sings so movingly, *The Colour of My Love* also offered Céline the opportunity to make a personal statement that she felt was long overdue. Released in late 1993, the album's acknowledgments included the following tribute: "René, for so many years I've kept our special dream locked away in my heart…but now it's getting too powerful to keep inside…so after all these years, let me 'paint the truth, show how I feel'…René, you're the color of my love."

In early December 1996, Céline appeared at the Billboard *Music Awards, where, astonishingly, she did not win an award.*

A Fairy Tale Wedding

Above: Céline had eight bridal attendants (her sisters) and René had eight groomsmen. The latter are shown here in their dapper top-hat-and-tails ensembles escorting the bride's mother, Thérèse, and the groom's mother, Alice, to the event.

Left: Wedded bliss at last! After years of secrecy, Céline and René finally publicized their union in the fall of 1993, marrying a year later in Montreal, on December 17, 1994.

Opposite: Céline and René share a kiss for photographers at their wedding on December 17, 1994. Céline's headpiece featured more than 2,000 Austrian crystals.

Once the truth was revealed, Céline was delighted to be able to talk about her feelings for René. Even Céline's mother approved, telling reporters, "René's the best man for my daughter....It doesn't matter that he's twenty-seven years older. He's a wonderful man."

Appearing on *The Tonight Show* with Jay Leno, Céline announced that she and René would be married. The couple lost no time in planning their wedding. On December 17, 1994, the two tied the knot at Montreal's magnificent Notre Dame Basilica, in front of four hundred guests. Céline's eight sisters acted as her bridesmaids, holding her thirty-foot (9m) train as she floated down the aisle to join René at the altar. At a press reception following the ceremony, Céline proclaimed her happiness, joking with reporters, and pretending to swoon into René's arms, telling him, "I love you so much." Later, at the reception, Céline danced with joy, and when her siblings gathered around to sing a song they had written just for her wedding, she wept with joy. A five-course meal was followed by an enormous wedding cake made of profiteroles. (Céline later confided to Larry King that it took 2,000 profiteroles to create her fantasy cake.)

It was the wedding she had fantasized about since she was a young girl—surrounded by her beloved family, wearing a dress fit for a princess, Céline had finally married the man who helped her to achieve her dreams.

CELINE'S WEDDING DRESS

Céline worked with Montreal-based designers Mirella and Steve Gentile on her magnificent wedding gown. Some facts:

Fabric: **Silk with lace, plus embroidered and beaded detailing**
Color: **Ivory**
Neckline: **Sweetheart**
Bodice: **Fitted**
Skirt: **Very full, with crinolines**
Sleeves: **Long, sheer, and lacy, extending to a point on the hand**
Train: **Thirty feet (9m) long, detachable**
Headpiece: **A sparkling crystal crown with waist-length veil attached**
Accessories: **A cropped white mink jacket**

Above: Céline credits René with much of her success; she is quick to praise him, frequently telling interviewers "I have the best management."

Left: Céline and René pose at Carnegie Hall in New York City where they attended a benefit for the Gay Men's Health Crisis on January 22, 1997.

Left: *On April 17, 1997, Céline and René were once again in Monaco for the World Music Awards, where Céline was presented with three awards: Best-selling Artist, Best-selling Pop Artist, and Best-selling Female Canadian singer.*

Above: *René suffered a heart attack in 1992, after which Céline insisted that life was too short to hide their love. Although their relationship quickly became an open secret, René persuaded Céline to wait a little while longer before making an official announcement. In 1993, with the launch of* The Colour of My Love, *they announced their upcoming wedding.*

Above: *Céline looks radiant as she poses for photographers at the Time for Peace Awards in New York City on November 17, 1997.*

Opposite: *Céline is pleased to receive a kiss along with her World Music Award from actor Jean-Claude Van Damme at the 1996 ceremony in Monaco.*

TITANIC SUCCESS

S tarting out 1995 with her dreams of love and success come true, Céline nevertheless wasted no time getting back to work. If she had needed any further proof of her popularity in the United States, it came when she was asked to perform at the inauguration of President Bill Clinton in Washington, D.C. The American fans reacted as enthusiastically as her die-hard Québécois admirers, letting Céline know that her voice could transcend all kinds of boundaries.

In the meantime, Sony had released a compilation album in French, *Les premières années* (The Early Years) and a live recording of Céline's triumphant Parisian performances, *Céline Dion à l'Olympia*. It was time to record again in French, and this time Céline worked with French recording star Jean-Jacques Goldman. The resulting disc, titled *D'eux*, topped the French pop charts, becoming the biggest seller ever in France. It was also released in English, as *The French Album*. In just one year, Céline had achieved number one hits in the United States, Canada, Britain, and France; it seemed she was on her way to conquering the world.

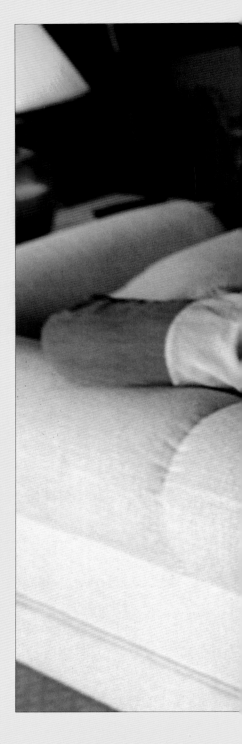

Above: *By March 1992, Céline was already a star in Canada and France, and was beginning to be known in the United States as well. That year, she won Female Singer of the Year at Canada's Juno Awards.*

Opposite: *In 1996, in recognition of her contributions to French cultural life, France's Ministry of Culture awarded Céline the prestigious title of* Chevalier de l'Ordre des Arts et des Lettres.

This 1996 photo from Céline's European tour reveals the massive stage set that formed the dramatic backdrop to her concert.

Falling into You

Sony had no desire to slow Céline's incredible trajectory toward megastardom: in 1995 they assembled a "dream team" of producers to work on her fourth English-language album. The superstar line-up included David Foster, Jim Steinman (of Meat Loaf fame), Todd Rundgren, Eric Carmen, Canadian Dan Hill, Aldo Nova, and astonishingly, the legendary Phil Spector.

Spector is as well known for his genius in the recording studio as he is for his difficult temperament. Famous for creating the multi-layered "Wall of Sound" effect, Spector had basically retired from producing, finding most of today's acts insufficiently interesting. However, having seen Céline perform on television, he felt that she had a talent worthy of his efforts. Typically, Spector insisted on exerting total control over his sessions with Céline. Such a situation was radically different from Céline's usual recording sessions, in which René always had a significant voice. Not surprisingly, they began almost immediately to clash, and Spector ultimately resigned. In a statement published in *Entertainment Weekly*, Spector complimented Céline but lashed out at the rest of the team, calling them "amateurs, students, and bad clones of yours truly." None of the material recorded with Spector was ever released; he is holding on to it. Fortunately, the other sessions went much better.

"Because You Loved Me" was the theme song for the Michelle Pfeiffer/Robert Redford

Céline was nominated in four categories at 1997's Grammys. She ultimately went home with two awards, both for Falling into You—*Best Pop Album and Album of the Year.*

weeper *Up Close and Personal*. Written by Diane Warren, whose songs Céline had recorded previously, "Because You Loved Me" was the first single from *Falling into You*. It promptly topped the charts, remaining at number one on *Billboard's* Adult Contemporary list for five straight months.

Jim Steinman both wrote and produced the truly spectacular "It's All Coming Back to Me Now," which, at some eight minutes long, surpassed the usual length of pop songs by quite a bit. (Steinman has an affinity for long, theatrical songs—he worked with Meat Loaf on "Paradise by the Dashboard Light.") A dramatic tour de force of a song, "It's All Coming Back to Me Now" suited Céline's style to a tee, and she reveled in the opportunity to really delve into its images of love lost and found. The video, which featured Céline in a suitably romantic setting (it was shot in a European castle), received frequent airings on both VH1 and MuchMusic; likewise, radio stations, undaunted by the song's length, put it into almost constant rotation.

On its release in March 1996, *Falling into You* vaulted into the number two spot (another Canadian songstress, Alanis Morisette, and her album *Jagged Little Pill*, refused to be dislodged from first place) on the U.S. charts. As the record was released around the world, it easily shot up to number one in England, France, and as far away as Australia. By September, it was in first place on the *Billboard* Hot 200, and it remained in the top five for twenty-seven consecutive weeks. *Falling into You* was the most successful release of Céline's career, and it helped to make her a household name world-

NOTABLE DUETS

"Wishful Thinking"
 with Dan Hill, on *True Love*, **1989**
"Beauty and the Beast"
 with Peabo Bryson, **1992**
"When I Fall in Love"
 with Clive Griffin, **1993**
"Plus haut que moi"
 (Higher Than Myself) with
 Mario Pelchat, on *Plus haut
 que moi,* **1993**
"Petit Papa Noël" with Alvin and
 the Chipmunks, on *A Very Merry
 Chipmunk,* **1994**
"Mejor decir adios" (It's Hard to Say
 Goodbye) with Paul Anka,
 on *Amigos,* **1996**
"Love Lights the World"
 with Peabo Bryson and
 Color Me Badd, on *For Our
 Children Too,* **1996**
"Tell Him," with Barbra Streisand, 1997
"I'm Your Angel," with R. Kelly, 1998
"The Prayer," with Andrea Bocelli, 1998

Opposite: *Gleaming in gold, Céline takes the mike and sings from the bottom of her heart.*

Below: *Céline has admired Barbra Streisand since childhood, and until recently, singing with her was just a dream—but the dream came true, and Céline says it was the pinnacle of her career.*

wide. (In fact, the record continues to sell, with a current total of more than twenty-four million copies sold around the world.) In 1996, it seemed only fitting that Céline, a true global superstar, sing at the opening ceremonies of that year's summer Olympics in Atlanta, Georgia.

And the Nominees Are

Although it came as no surprise when "Because You Loved Me" was nominated for Best Original Song, Céline was very excited to be asked to sing at 1997's Academy Awards. By now a veteran Oscar show performer, Céline was nevertheless thrilled by the glamour of attending Hollywood's most star-studded event.

Among the competition that year was Barbra Streisand's song from *The Mirror Has Two Faces*, "I Finally Found Someone." Denied nominations in both the star and director categories, Streisand had reportedly refused to sing her song at the award ceremony, so Nathalie Cole was asked to substitute for her. When Cole called in sick the day before the show, the frantic producers asked Céline to do both numbers.

Long an admirer of Streisand, Céline was at once elated and anxious, especially when she discovered, shortly before going on, that Streisand herself was in the audience. What Céline did not know was that Barbra had actually left the auditorium just as Céline was about to take the stage. The official story was that nature had called; the tabloid papers speculated more unkindly that Barbra could not bear to hear the younger woman sing her song. Whatever the truth, Céline performed both songs magnificently, and the audience in the Shrine Auditorium responded with great warmth to her efforts. The evening was a triumph—made so much sweeter when Céline

Above: *Céline clutches one of her three World Music Awards at the 1996 ceremony in Monaco. Princess Stephanie and Prince Albert of Monaco, at whose table Céline was seated for dinner, also attended the awards.*

Opposite: *Arriving at the 1997 Oscars, Céline stopped to chat with Courtney Love.*

received a bouquet of flowers and a note from Barbra a few days later, congratulating Céline on her performance, and adding, "Next time, let's do one together."

In the awards category, it was a banner year for Céline. Already a record-breaker in Canadian music awards (for years she had dominated both the French and English music competitions), in 1997 Céline was asked to perform at the Grammy Awards in New York City. With David Foster on piano, Céline took the stage at Madison Square Garden and belted out "Because You Loved Me." That night Céline went home with two Grammy Awards—*Falling into You* had won Best Pop Album and Album of the Year. Céline's total 1997 winnings consisted of two Grammys, four Junos, five Félix Awards, and four World Music Awards!

The only question was: where could Céline go from here?

Above: *Céline arrives at the 1997 Academy Awards, dressed in a shimmering Christian Dior dress and dramatic Chanel diamond necklace. She shows not a trace of nerves, despite her upcoming unprecedented two-song performance.*

The Heart of the Matter

The answer came from Jim Horner, with whom Céline had worked on the never-released tune for Spielberg's *Fievel* sequel. Horner was now working on *Titanic*, a movie that had been generating gossip almost since the day work had begun on it. Directed by Canadian-born James Cameron (of *Terminator* fame), *Titanic* had a stupendous and ever-increasing budget of some $200 million, a special effects challenge of enormous proportions, two young stars (only one well-known, Leonardo DiCaprio), and was plagued by delays. The film was considered a dubious prospect by many in Hollywood. Only Cameron remained unwavering in his faith in *Titanic*—and exercised iron control over every aspect of its making. Although Cameron had insisted that pop tunes were out of the question for this film, Horner believed that a well-written love song would add something special to the movie's emotional impact and he secretly commissioned a song.

Horner presented "My Heart Will Go On" to René and Céline as a song that would have to be recorded in secret. Moved by the song and impressed with Horner's commitment to it, Céline agreed to record a demo for Cameron to hear when the time was right. Weeks later, Horner played "My Heart Will Go On" for Cameron, who recognized right away that the song was ideal for *Titanic*. Interestingly, "My Heart Will Go On" was not re-recorded; the song we hear on the soundtrack is Céline's

Céline pauses for the cameras outside the Dorothy Chandler Pavilion before the 1997 Academy Awards. Céline's necklace had more than six hundred individual diamonds forming a star with a comet-like tail.

At the Academy Awards ceremony, after "My Heart Will Go On" won the award for Best Original Song, Céline shared a triumphant moment with composer James Horner and lyricist Will Jennings.

Above: *Wearing clothes by Chanel, one of her favorite designers, Céline posed for photographers in Monaco, where she was attending the World Music Awards.*

Opposite: *Céline looks very excited to be attending the World Music Awards in Monaco, 1996.*

original rendition. In an interview in *USA Weekend*, she recalled that during the recording session, which took place before Céline had seen any of the movie, Horner described the events to her—the old couple who choose to die in each others' arms, the mother reading her children a last goodnight story, and the enduring love shared by Rose and Jack. Céline wept, "I took the emotions of everyone. I became it all." Those waves of emotion came through so clearly in Céline's singing, she captured so completely the mood of the epic love story, that the song needed no reworking. "My Heart Will Go On" provided a powerfully poignant finale to the film.

The story of *Titanic*'s triumph is well known by now: it became one of the most successful movies ever, breaking records around the world, making a megastar of its lead actor, and transforming its director into the self-described "king of the world." The story of Jack and Rose won the hearts of movie-goers around the world, many of whom saw it multiple times. "My Heart Will Go On" debuted at number one on *Billboard's* singles chart. Just a month after the movie was released, "My Heart Will Go On" had become one of the most-requested songs ever.

Céline told BBC Radio interviewer Richard Allison, "The songs I pick, they're full of emotion."

Let's Talk About Love

In addition to being included on *Titanic's* soundtrack, "My Heart Will Go On" also appeared on Céline's next album, 1997's *Let's Talk About Love*. A departure from her previous albums, *Let's Talk About Love* contained a number of songs that saw Céline joining forces with some of our era's greatest voices.

Intrigued by Barbra Streisand's post-Academy Awards invitation to Céline, René had asked David Foster, who had worked with both singers, to try to make it a reality. Each a major star in her own right, the two women recording together would be an historic occasion. Céline had long idolized Barbra and was utterly thrilled when the legendary singer agreed to the duet. David Foster, his wife, Linda Thomson, and producer Walter Afanasieff wrote "Tell Him" expressly for Barbra and Céline—it features a young woman asking a more experienced friend for advice about an *affaire du coeur*. Shaking with excitement, Céline went into the studio feeling that despite all her accomplishments, this would be the most exciting day of her career.

The recording went beautifully, the two women clearly enjoyed working together. Herb Ritts had been called in to photograph the momentous session, and captured Barbra and Céline's mutual admiration on film. Céline has since described the experience as the musical pinnacle of her life. She told Larry King that she admires Streisand for "her singing, her beauty,

Left: *In May 1996, Céline attended the World Music Awards in Monaco. She was honored there for having sold more albums around the world (twenty million-plus) in 1995 than any other Canadian artist.*

Opposite: *Céline at the 38th Annual Grammy Awards ceremony in 1996.*

and her strength," and confessed that singing with her was "a dream come true."

Streisand was not the only legendary talent to appear on *Let's Talk About Love*. Producer George Martin, renowned for his groundbreaking work with The Beatles and recently knighted, came on board to produce "The Reason," a collaboration between Céline and chart-topping singer-songwriter Carole King. With a long list of hit songs, King's songwriting genius is indisputable. Her singing accomplishments are also formidable, with the ten—million-plus selling *Tapestry* album a testament to her popularity. Despite her own success, King noted that as a songwriter, it would give her great pleasure to hear a singer of Céline's talent perform her song. King herself would do back-up vocals. Of the sessions that produced "The Reason," Sir George said simply, "It was a high."

On any list of the most impressive singing talent in the world today, the name of legendary tenor Luciano Pavarotti would no doubt be found at the top. Céline might have had to pinch herself the morning she woke up to find a recording session with Pavarotti on her schedule. *Let's Talk About Love* includes the Dion-Pavarotti duet, "I Hate You Then I Love You." Céline reportedly felt awed by the opportunity to sing with Pavarotti and thrilled at the way their collaboration turned out. In 1998, she was gratified to be asked to appear with Pavarotti in a benefit concert for refugee children, "Pavarotti and Friends." The show also featured The Spice Girls, which is how the unlikely combination of the British girl band and Céline came to be on an album together.

Moving from opera to disco may be a stretch for many singers, but given the opportunity to

CELINE'S ACTING CAREER

In 1991, Céline actually starred in a made-for-television movie filmed for the Canadian Broadcasting Corporation (CBC). The movie, *Des fleurs sur la neige* (*Flowers in the Snow*), stars Céline as a troubled young woman who struggles with the memories of child abuse, especially when she decides to start a family of her own. Since then, Céline has made cameo appearances on several television shows, including *The Nanny* in 1997 and *Touched by an Angel* in 1998. She also appeared on *Sesame Street* in October 1998.

Céline has said that she would like to star in a movie about the life of the famed French singer Edith Piaf.

add The Bee Gees to the star-studded list of contributors to *Let's Talk About Love*, Céline and René did not hesitate. The brothers Gibb—Maurice, Robin, and Barry—actually wrote a song for Céline, which they titled "Immortality." United in their admiration for her, the brothers declared after the session that Céline's rendition of their song brought tears to their eyes. Céline herself noted how proud she was to have been chosen by them to sing such a special song.

Finally, believing that artistic growth comes only with risk, Céline worked with R&B artist Diana King on a dance tune called "Treat Her like a Lady," as well as the Spanish-language "Amar haciendo el amor" to complete *Let's Talk About Love*. Exhilarated by the experience of working with such incredible writing, producing, and singing talent, Céline called the album the best work of her life.

Released in late 1997, *Let's Talk About Love* debuted at number two in the United States and in the top position in Canada, Britain, Australia, and France. Demand for the album was so intense that Sony could barely keep up with it. The year 1998 opened triumphantly for Céline—her risk-taking had paid off spectacularly.

Céline and René smile for the cameras at a party in December 1996. At the end of 1996, VH1 named Céline Artist of the Year.

Céline has toured constantly ever since she was a child and has garnered fans all over the world. Here she performs in Brussels, Belgium, where 60,000 fans turned out to see her June 20, 1997, concert.

On Top of the World

A "global diva" (so labeled by *Time* magazine) by 1998, Céline had become one the most popular singers in the world. Her international fans were clamoring for a visit from their idol in person, and in March, she announced a major, two-year world tour. Fans were ecstatic and ticket sales took off immediately.

Meanwhile, the producers of the 1998 Grammy Awards were hoping to put together a spectacular show by recreating the Streisand/Dion magic live. Céline excitedly announced

Opposite: *In 1996, Céline's* Falling into You *tour saw her perform more than 110 concerts worldwide. In late March, she visited Australia and New Zealand, where she gave nine shows. Here, she wows fans at Sydney's Entertainment Center.*

Below: *Clad in black leather, Céline sang at the MIDEM Awards in France, where she was honored as the best-selling artist of all time in France, with combined sales in 1996 of more than ten million albums.*

Above: At the 39th Annual Grammy Awards, held at New York City's Madison Square Garden on February 26, 1997, Céline performed "Because You Loved Me," accompanied by producing legend David Foster on piano.

Opposite: Outside the Four Seasons Hotel in New York City, where GMHC Benefit attendees enjoyed dinner, Céline pauses for photographers.

the forthcoming duet (the two would sing "Tell Him") on *The Oprah Winfrey Show*—but she was devastated just a week later when the flu put Barbra out of commission. Ever the trouper, Céline took the stage solo, to deliver a gorgeous version of "My Heart Will Go On." (She did it again at 1998's Academy Awards, when *Titanic* swept almost every category.) In an interview with *McCall's* magazine, Streisand spoke of her warm regard for Céline, declaring, "Céline is all anyone could ask for in a singing partner—professional, easygoing, generous... her amazing voice is surpassed only by her kind and gentle heart."

The popular music channel VH1 counts Céline among its top draws and focused on her as April 1998's VH1 Artist of the Month. On April 14, in a spectacular event that was billed as VH1's Divas Live, Céline joined Canadian country star Shania Twain, along with Queen of Soul Aretha Franklin, pop sensation Mariah Carey, and international superstar Gloria Estefan at New York's Beacon Theater for a star-powered evening of song.

It had been some time since Céline had recorded in French, so in 1998 she joined forces once again with French star Jean-Jacques Goldman to make the album, *S'il suffisait d'aimer* (If Love Were Enough). Drawing on a broader range of influences, the material on *S'il suffisait d'aimer* reveals Céline's depth and versatility—and a growing maturity. Blues, soul, and intimate songs dominate this album, prompting several reviewers to recommend it to Céline's English-speaking listeners as "a must-have for any true fan."

Above: *Céline performing at the Jingle Ball at New York City's Madison Square Garden in December 1997.*

Opposite: *The Lady in Red: Céline acknowledged her enthusiastic audience at the Jingle Ball, held in New York City on December 9, 1997. In just ten days, the movie* Titanic *would be released, and "My Heart Will Go On" would become the most-requested radio song of the year.*

These Are Special Times

Although Céline enjoys the work of recording, not to mention the excitement of meeting and performing with other entertainers, she has always been quick to explain that her greatest pleasure comes from singing live, sharing her voice and her songs with her fans. The World Tour has offered her an opportunity to really connect with her audience, and no expense or care was spared in planning the show. The stage set is a phenomenon in itself. An illuminated heart outline defines the stage area, within which are four mini-stages, several of which are powered by special hydraulic lifts so they can rise above the main heart for certain songs. Céline's backup includes three singers and nine musicians.

Designed to showcase her versatility as a performer as well as make sure the fans get to hear their favorites, the show includes moments both intimate and sensational. Starting off the show with a fan favorite, local children's choirs are recruited to perform backup on "Let's Talk About Love." Their presence supplies a special hometown touch to each concert, not to mention a never-to-be-forgotten experience for the kids themselves.

Céline was anxious to include some songs that had special meaning for her, so she has a selection of tunes that are personal favorites, including The Beatles' "Because" and Eric Clapton's "Tears in Heaven." Particularly moving are Céline's subtle take on Roberta Flack's

Above: *Looking elegant in an all-white pantsuit, Céline sang "Treat Her like a Lady" at the* Essence *Awards on May 21, 1998.*

Opposite: *At the 1997 World Music Awards Céline gave a rousing performance of "Call the Man," backed up by a gospel group.*

Pictured here with Big Bird, Elmo, and Harry in 1997, Céline is a repeat guest of Sesame Street. *In 1998, she sang "Happy to Meet You," which can be seen and heard on the* Elmopalooza *video.*

"The First Time Ever I Saw Your Face," and a Sinatra song that she describes as special to her and René, "All the Way."

Paying tribute to The Bee Gees, whose "Immortality" appeared on *Let's Talk About Love,* Céline does a spectacular disco-inspired medley, complete with mirrored ball and lights. Her renditions of "Staying Alive" and "You Should Be Dancing," which includes a parody of Travolta's white-suited disco strut, bring the crowd to its feet every time.

Special effects on the tour include video duets with Barbra Streisand ("Tell Him") and Diane King ("Treat Her like a Lady"). And for the heart-stopping finale, Céline performs "My Heart Will Go On" braced against the prow of a ship that rises from the stage.

Fans who are unable to see Céline live got great news when it was announced that a video of her August 1998 Memphis concert was filmed. *Live in Memphis* was released in November 1998, and contains footage of Céline performing "Twist and Shout."

In October, Céline took some time to help the folks at *Sesame Street* celebrate their thirtieth anniversary. She sang "Happy to Meet You," which appears on *Elmopalooza.*

Then, just in time for the holidays, Céline filmed her first television special, a holiday show entitled *These Are Special Times.* Taking viewers on a nostalgic journey to her home town of Charlemagne, Quebec, Céline introduced her family and shared some of their special holiday traditions. The show also included guest appearances by talk show host Rosie O'Donnell and Italian tenor Andrea Bocelli. In December, the disc of *These Are Special Times* was released to rave reviews. Once again a group of

Above: *Céline and tenor Andrea Bocelli gave a moving performance on* These Are Special Times.

Above, left: *Céline caught in a casual moment at a rehearsal for the Grammys in February 1998.*

Left: *Céline has fans everywhere. Here she greets Marla Maples, ex-wife of real-estate magnate Donald Trump, backstage at the Paramount Theater in New York on July 29, 1996. On February 23 of the same year Céline gave a private concert for Trump.*

top-notch producers, including David Foster, Bryan Adams, Ric Wake, and R. Kelly, brought their unique talents to the recording. Demonstrating her versatility, Céline received a co-writing credit on the song "Don't Save It All for Christmas Day." The album's other highlights include "I'm Your Angel," a duet with R. Kelly; "The Prayer," the song Céline sang on the television special with Andrea Bocelli; as well as "Another Year Has Gone By," a song written by Bryan Adams for Céline.

Billboard called *These Are Special Times* "no ordinary holiday project." The reviewer continued, "Sounding completely at ease and wielding a wildly creative wand, an ever-maturing Dion conjures up surprise after surprise." Within a month of the album's release, it appeared at the top of *Billboard's* Christmas Album Chart and in the number three spot on the Hot 200.

By the end of 1998, the accolades for Céline had reached new heights: she was the winner of MuchMusic's People's Choice Award; the Recording Industry of America had named her Best-Selling Artist of the Year; she was VH1's Artist of the Year (for the second time); and had won six Billboard Music awards.

1999 would be no different. On January 10, at the People's Choice Award Ceremony, she was named Favorite Female Music Performer. She received two Grammys, including awards for Record of the Year and Best Female Pop Vocal Performance, both for "My Heart Will Go On."

Above: Céline was a guest performer for Luciano Pavarotti's benefit concert for the children of Liberia in June 1998. She is pictured here with the Spice Girls, Sporty, Baby, Posh, and Scary (Ginger had already left the band).

Opposite: Céline poses with Wyclef Jean at the rehearsals for the 1998 Grammy Awards.

Above left: In addition to her big hits, Céline's 1998 Let's Talk About Love *tour featured some personal favorites, including The Beatles'"Because" and Eric Clapton's "Tears in Heaven."*

Above: Céline began her Let's Talk About Love *world tour in 1998; here she is belting out a song in concert in San Jose, California, in October. Her outfit is designed by Christian Lacroix.*

Opposite: 1998 began an intensive two-year world tour for Céline. Here she gives her Washington, D.C., audience the thumbs up.

Right: *Céline and René arrive at the 70th Annual Academy Awards in Los Angeles in 1998.*

Opposite: *Céline performs in Washington, D.C., in August 1998. "It makes me happy when I'm onstage and my voice is in its top shape and I can sing my songs without thinking about techniques...when I enjoy every moment, then the...fans are happy and it makes me happy."*

Singing/songwriting
legend Carole King wrote
(and did vocals with
Céline for) "The Reason"
on Let's Talk About Love;
she also joined Céline
onstage during the
VH1-sponsored
Divas Live concert.

Above: *Until just two days before the show, Céline and Barbra Streisand were planning to perform "Tell Him" live at the Grammys—unfortunately, Barbra fell ill and could not attend. Never one to disappoint her fans, Céline went on solo with a crowd-pleasing rendition of "My Heart Will Go On."*

Opposite: *Céline in France in 1998 where she has been a star since the mid-eighties. She has filled ever-larger venues in concert, has won numerous honors, and holds several records for best-selling albums and singles. In December 1998, Paris Match named her Woman of the Year.*

MILLENNIUM CELINE

With her world tour taking her overseas through 1999, Céline will wrap it up back home with a concert on New Year's Eve at Montreal's Molson Centre. Then, she and René are planning to take some richly deserved time off to be together—and maybe start the family that Céline has yearned for. Since their marriage, Céline has spoken frankly of her desire to start a family and her concern that her grueling schedule (and resulting thinness (Céline carries only 115 [52.3 kg] pounds on her 5'7" [170 cm] frame) may prevent her from conceiving. She frequently jokes with reporters about she and René having fun "trying" or "practicing" for a family, but there has been an undertone of sadness. After a poll reported that 82 percent of her fans surveyed said that they would like Céline to take a break and have a baby, Céline spoke ruefully to an interviewer for USA Weekend, "I love that 82 percent…they want me to rest, but they all have tickets to my show!"

René told *USA Today* that he shares Céline's desire for a more normal lifestyle, noting, "after this tour, I want her to stop for at least two years." Céline agreed, proclaiming, "I can't wait to go grocery shopping and drive my car." Fans can rest assured that she will be back. Céline has said that she does not want to stop her career completely and she has mentioned the possibility of doing some film work, including, possibly, a movie about the life of Edith Piaf; she and Barbra Streisand have even spoken of working together on a film.

Céline is proud of her accomplishments, and deeply grateful to have been welcomed so warmly into the hearts of her many fans. She believes that one reason her songs of love have struck such a chord is that people today "are in need of love and attention"—and if her singing gives them pleasure, her own happiness is increased. Céline's love of singing is so deep that it has defined her since childhood and propelled her to stardom; coupled with her strong sense of warmth toward her fans, it will ensure that no matter what else her future holds, she will always lift that heavenly voice in song, to the joy of all who hear her.

CELINE'S FAN CLUB

If you would like to join Céline's official fan club, write to:
Céline Dion International Fan Club
P.O. Box 551
Don Mills, Ontario
M3C 2T6

Above: *Céline with the staff at a Nickels restaurant in Canada. Céline and René are among the founding members of the Nickels restaurant chain, which has spread throughout Ontario and Quebec since the first restaurant was opened in January 1990.*

Discography

FRENCH

1998 *S'il suffisait d'aimer*

This recording marks Céline's second collaboration with French superstar Jean-Jacques Goldman.

1997 *C'est pour vivre*

A compilation that includes six songs not previously released on CD.

1996 *Live à Paris*

These songs were recorded at Céline's Paris concerts in October 1995.

1995 *D'eux*

(Released in the U.S. as *The French Album*) Céline's first collaboration with Jean Jacques Goldman, *D'eux* is to date the best-selling French album ever in both Quebec and France.

1994 *Céline Dion à l'Olympia*

Recorded during Céline's triumphant Olympia series in September 1994.

1993 *Les premières années*

A compilation of Céline's early songs.

1991 *Dion chante Plamodon*

Céline sings the songs of Québécois composer Luc Plamodon.

1988 *The Best of Céline Dion / Vivre*

A compilation album of Céline's greatest hits, released only in Europe.

1987 *Incognito*

Céline's first album for Sony.

1986 *Les chansons en or*

A collection of Céline's biggest hits to date.

1985 *Céline Dion en concert*

This is Céline's first live album, recorded in May 1985 at Place des Arts in Montreal.

C'est pour toi

This was the last album Céline recorded before her "sabbatical" to learn English and change her style.

1984 *Les plus grands succès de Céline Dion*

A portion of the profits from this album were donated to the Cystic Fibrosis Foundation.

Mélanie

Les oiseaux de bonheur

1983 *Chants et contes de Noël*

Les chemins de ma maison

Du soleil au coeur

1982 *Tellement j'ai d'amour*

This album brought Céline her first gold record in Quebec.

1981 *La voix du bon Dieux*

Céline chante Noël

These were Céline's very first recordings, masterminded (and funded) by René.

ENGLISH

1990 *Unison*

Céline's first English-language album, which sold more than 600,000 units in Canada alone and almost 2 million worldwide.

1992 *Céline Dion*

Céline's second English album, her first to go platinum in the United States, with four hit singles.

1993 *The Colour of My Love*

A solid hit, this album confirmed Céline's star status.

1996 *Falling Into You*

Céline's first album to reach number one on the Billboard charts. Gold, Volumes I and II

COLLECTIONS OF CELINE'S GREATEST HITS

1997 *Let's Talk About Love*

Céline's fifth album in English topped charts around the world.

The Collection 1982–88

This is a two-CD set of Céline's early recordings.

1998 *These Are Special Times*

Céline's holiday tunes, released to accompany a television special.

SOUNDTRACK SONGS

1985 *The Peanut Butter Solution*

(Operation beurre de pinottes): "Listen to the Magic," "Michael's Song"

1989 *Listen to Me:* "Listen to Me"

1992 *Beauty and the Beast:* "Beauty and the Beast" (with Peabo Bryson)

1993 *Sleepless in Seattle:* "When I Fall in Love" (with Clive Griffen)

1996 *Up Close and Personal:* "Because You Loved Me"

1997 *Titanic:* "My Heart Will Go On"

Bibliography

BOOKS:

Richard Crouse. *A Voice and a Dream: The Céline Dion
　　Story*. New York: Ballantine Books, 1998
Ian Halperin. *Céline Dion: Behind the Fairy Tale*.
　　Boca Raton: Boca Publications Group, 1997

ARTICLES AND INTERVIEWS:

Jennifer Graham, *TV Guide*, November 18, 1998
Edna Gundersen, *USA Today*, August 21, 1998
Mary Lamey, *Montreal Gazette*, September 9, 1998
Jeffrey Zaslow, *USA Weekend*, September 11–13, 1998

REVIEWS:

Billboard, November 7, 1998: *These Are Special Times*
Billboard, September 4, 1998: Madison Square Garden
　　concert
Boston Phoenix, October 22, 1998: *S'il suffisait d'aimer*

WEBSITES:

Passion Céline Dion www.celine-dion.net/
www.geocities.com/~c-e-l-i-n-e
Sony official site: celineonline.com

*January 10, 1999, saw Céline win the People's Choice
Award as Favorite Female Music Performer.*

Index

Photography Credits